Little Acts of

Bravery

COUNTLESS WAYS TO
BOOST YOUR CONFIDENCE

This edition published in 2019
By SJG Publishing, HP22 6NF, UK

Author: Rebecca Dickinson
Cover design: Milestone Creative
Contents design: seagulls.net

ISBN: 978-1-911517-72-6

Printed in China

10 9 8 7 6 5 4 3 2 1

'Be who you
are and say
what you feel,
because those
who mind
don't matter,
and those who
matter don't
mind.'

Dr. Seuss

Introduction

Be brave! Never have two words been so
easy to say, but so difficult to act on.

It can often appear that some people
are naturally endowed with lashings of
self-confidence. Often, these are the people
who were always the star of the school
play, the captain of the sports team,
or the life and soul of the party.

But appearances aren't everything; self-confidence isn't about being loud and extrovert, the first in the line, or even the most successful. True self-confidence means being comfortable with who you are and letting go of the fears and insecurities that prevent you from doing the things you want to do and being the person you want to be.

When you are brave enough to believe in yourself, others are more likely to believe in you too. Research shows that people who feel good about themselves get treated in ways that reinforce that self-belief, leading to greater self-esteem.

Whether it's walking on a tightrope, handling a fearsome snake, standing up to someone who's abused you, or finally asking the person you've secretly admired for months out for a drink, bravery comes from within. It's about having the guts to try, regardless of the outcome. And then trying again.

The road to self-confidence also involves acknowledging our flaws, and those of others, and refusing to be held back by them. Yet often, it's our own fear of failure, or of being judged, that prevents us from trying new things or seeking happiness.

Sometimes these fears are so deep rooted, stemming from a profound lack of self-worth, that it's necessary to seek professional help. This book isn't a substitute for therapy, but a tool to help you become the person you want to be, rather than the person you are afraid to be.

The acts of bravery in this book will gently push your boundaries and encourage you to realize your full potential. They range from the fun and frivolous to the more serious and soul-searching. You will also find research-based techniques for overcoming fears and self-doubt. Whatever you do, whatever your story, be brave!

Face the Fear

You'll never know how brave you are until you confront the monsters under the bed. (They may not be as scary as you think.)

I Fear

THEREFORE I AM

The truth is we are all afraid.

Fear is normal and universal – it's part of what makes us human. It's the brain's way of protecting us and ensuring the survival of the species. Fear is what keeps us away from the edge.

Early humans needed the fast, powerful 'fight or flight' responses triggered by fear, to keep them safe. Although we no longer face the same threats of physical danger as our ancestors, our minds and bodies still work in the same way.

'It is not the mountain we conquer but ourselves.'

Edmund Hillary

The fear response is part of our genetic heritage. The trouble is that it can kick in when we are confronted with non-dangerous modern-day worries such as money, work, relationships and social situations.

So while fear is a useful response if you're confronted by a venomous snake, it's less useful if you're confronted by your boss. And it's nothing but a nuisance when it gets in the way of activities such as taking exams, speaking in public, standing up for your beliefs, or meeting new people.

Bravery, on the other hand, is what happens when we learn to stop letting fear *inter-fear* with our lives. So let's get started...

Know when to seek help: if fear and anxiety impact on your everyday life then consult a doctor or therapist for advice.

WHAT IS BRAVERY?

It would be easy to assume that bravery is an absence of fear. In fact, it's quite the opposite. Bravery is about feeling the fear and doing it anyway: the soldier who marches into battle, the rape victim who stands up in court, the child who turns off the bedside light.

Bravery is having the strength to act, speak or think when every cell in your body is screaming 'stop!' It's about making a conscious effort to rise above your fears in order to be the person you want to be and live the life you want. Bravery is what happens when we don't give in to fear.

What's more, being brave makes us happy! As well as propelling us toward our goals, bravery plays a huge role in the way we feel about ourselves, filling us with self-confidence and pride. Without bravery in our lives we are left with shame and regret. So it's time to dig deep and start living to the max.

'The purpose of life is to live it, to taste experience to the utmost, to reach out eagerly and without fear for newer and richer experience.'

Eleanor Roosevelt

TAKE OFF THE STABILIZERS!

Think back to the time in your childhood when you learnt how to ride a bike (or another first, if you have yet to conquer that milestone.) Try to recapture the thrill of realizing you were pedalling without anybody holding on for the very first time. That's bravery! As adults, bravery is about having the guts to remove the stabilizers of life and ride without looking back. Of course, we will wobble and fall off at times, but we will also have the courage to get back on.

'Life shrinks or expands in proportion to one's courage'

Anaïs Nin

LITTLE ACTS OF BRAVERY
FOR BEGINNERS

As with any new skill, bravery takes practice, so here are a few suggestions to help you start flexing those muscles.

- Say 'hello' to five people you've never spoken to before.

- Make eye contact with people when you speak to them.

- Make an appointment to see a doctor about an embarrassing health complaint you've been putting off for ages.

- Go to the dentist – nobody really likes doing this, but it's worth conquering anxiety for the sake of your teeth.

- Pay a compliment to somebody you don't know very well.

- Ask a stranger if you can stroke their dog. Top marks if you're nervous about dogs.

LITTLE ACTS OF BRAVERY

Just for Fun

- Wear fancy dress for a whole day (not Halloween) while carrying out your normal activities. No hiding indoors!

- Watch a scary movie with all the lights off.

- Go horse riding.

- Ride a rollercoaster.

- Go skinny-dipping, as long as it's appropriate to do so.

- Roll all the way down a steep hill. Bonus points if you have an audience.

- Do a cartwheel in the park - it doesn't matter if anyone sees you!

THE TOOLS OF BRAVERY

Now you've warmed up with a few simple and fun acts of bravery, it's time to push yourself a little further. But first, you'll need some survival tips. The next few pages will equip you with some tried and tested techniques to help you summon up courage when you need it most. Use them like armor as you step bravely into battle.

'You will never do anything in this world without courage. It is the greatest quality in the mind next to honor.'

Aristotle

Relax

Many of us live such hectic lives and are in such a constant state of high-alert that we forget how it feels to truly relax. This progressive relaxation technique works by releasing physical tension, one muscle group at a time. It can also help you to have a better night's sleep. Aim to practice every evening or whenever you need to relax; you'll soon learn how a tense muscle feels compared to one that is completely relaxed.

- Lie or sit in a comfortable position. Take some slow, deep breaths, noticing your stomach rising, and your lungs filling with air. Do this for a couple of minutes.

- Starting with your toes, squeeze all the muscles as tightly as you can and hold for 5-10 seconds. Don't hold your breath – keep breathing in and out.

- Abruptly release the muscles and feel the tension melt away as you exhale. You might want to imagine a wave of relaxation washing over you.

- Move on to your left leg, drawing your toes upwards to feel the tension in your calf muscles. Hold for 5-10 seconds, then release. Do the same for your thigh muscles, then move on to your right leg.

- Continue to work up through the muscles of your body, one area at a time: buttocks, stomach, lower back, shoulders, arms and so on, right up to your face. As you exhale, imagine the tension being released and flowing away.

- Try to stay focused on your body the whole time. If your mind wanders, just return your attention to the muscle you are working on.

Affirmations

Give yourself a good talking to! Affirmations are short statements which are intended to rewire our brains and encourage positive thoughts. By regularly and confidently repeating an inner mantra to yourself such as 'I am confident and in control', it's possible to influence your subconscious mind and combat negative thoughts and fears. It may sound silly, but affirmations are a tried and tested technique, widely used by therapists, with proven success.

The technique works by programming your mind into believing the statement. This helps to break patterns of negative thoughts, which in turn helps to stop negative behavior and bring about positive changes in your life. As well as saying the affirmations out loud, it can also help to write them down several times in a notebook, or onto cards that you can carry around.

HEARING IS
Believing

Try repeating any of the affirmations below, or come up with your own personal ones. The important thing is to say them with conviction.

- Confident people make the most out of life. I choose to be confident.

- Life is an adventure. I can handle anything.

- I am the architect of my own life. I lay the foundations and make steady the walls.

- My dreams are coming true and obstacles are melting away.

- I am strong and calm.

- Today, I throw off old habits and begin new, positive ones.

Visualization

Did you know that just by imagining yourself achieving one of your goals, you can actually help make that goal a reality? Visualization involves 'watching' a mental image of yourself doing something you aspire to. The technique is often used by athletes and successful people to improve performance. It's not as crazy as it sounds: scientific studies show that visualization works by increasing motivation, coordination and concentration and reducing fear. This is because when we visualize an activity, it triggers our cells to act as if we are actually doing that activity, creating memories and learned behaviors – all without moving a muscle!

You don't need to be an Olympian or a high-flying business executive to practice visualization; you can use it to help prepare for all sorts of situations in which you experience fear and anxiety.

SEEING IS BELIEVING!

Do try this at home.

- Imagine sitting in a cinema, watching yourself achieving your goal in a movie – it could be anything from running a marathon to choosing salad over fries.

- Get up and enter the screen, so that you are actually present in the movie, rather than simply watching – this heightens the impact of the experience.

- See everything in vivid detail, engaging all your senses. What can you feel? What can you hear?

- Take it slowly – to be effective, you need to visualize every step of the process, in real time if possible. Envision pulling on your trainers, noticing the way they smell as you tighten the laces, feeling the material hug your feet.

- Practice – the more you use visualization, the more effective the technique becomes.

BE BRAVE, BE
Positive!

As we've discovered, fear can be a normal reaction when faced with a challenge. The goal is not to eliminate those fears but to change the way we react to them – and even to welcome them!

Instead of being paralyzed by fear, try to turn it into something positive. Fearful thoughts only make you more scared, whereas positive ones build courage.

- When you feel afraid, tell yourself: 'this fear will pass.'

- Instead of worrying about what could go wrong, say to yourself: 'wouldn't it be wonderful if...'

- Recognize your fears as a chance for personal growth.

- **Test yourself** – if you avoid situations that scare you, you'll never know whether something is as bad as you imagine and you'll miss out on what could have been. Exposing yourself to your fears is an effective way of overcoming them.

- **Know yourself** – keep a diary in which to note down your fears and anxieties and when they happen. Once you understand your underlying beliefs you can try to address them.

- **Relax** – as well as the progressive relaxation technique we've already looked at, try yoga, mindfulness or meditation. For a 'quick fix' take deep, slow breaths, or imagine yourself in a beautiful, soothing environment. There are also lots of great relaxation apps, such as Headspace.

'Stand up and face your fears, or they will defeat you.'

LL Cool J

'I've had a lot of worries in my life, most of which never happened.'

Mark Twain

RELEASE YOUR FEARS

In the words of a brave Disney princess: 'let it go!'

* Write down your fears on a sheet of paper then screw it up or burn it.

* Try the Guatemalan tradition of transferring your fears onto some worry dolls, then placing them under your pillow at night.

* Set aside a specific 'worry time' each day. This is known as 'stimulus control.' The idea is that by allowing yourself a designated period of time to think about your fears, you free up the rest of the day for positive thoughts and actions.

* Acknowledge your fears and express them out loud. Say: 'I feel scared.' Recognizing your feelings, instead of trying to dismiss them, can make them more manageable.

LITTLE ACTS OF BRAVERY TO MAKE YOU FEEL MORE EMPOWERED

Fear is like a prison. We shut ourselves away in order to avoid the prospect of failing, or getting hurt, or looking stupid. Yet in doing so we risk shutting ourselves off from the best that life has to offer.

Do any of these common fears sound familiar? If so try confronting some of them head-on.

- Apologize. It takes courage to admit when we're in the wrong.

- Share your opinion even if others disagree.

- Don't allow someone to take advantage of you.

- Accept an invitation to a party or an event.

- Ask someone who owes you money to pay you back.

- Call someone instead of texting.

'The secret to happiness is freedom… And the secret to freedom is courage.'

Thucydides

Brave New You

It's time to find your
inner tiger and let it roar.

MIRROR, MIRROR ON THE WALL

One of the biggest enemies of bravery is our own self-esteem, and sadly this is often rooted in physical appearance. Many of us judge ourselves with the harshest of rule books. What's more, we assume that because we judge ourselves, others judge us, too. Yet the truth is nobody notices your big nose, double chin, sticky-out ears or bushy eyebrows half as much as you do. And if they do, they need to work on themselves!

When we pay attention to our perceived flaws, we become weighed down with negative thoughts which can prevent us from embracing opportunity. Perhaps we even believe that only beautiful people can be successful.

Learning to accept yourself, and your imperfections, is one of the bravest acts of all. So step away from the mirror and leap into life!

Little Acts
OF SELF-ACCEPTANCE

- **Hold your head up high** – look in front of you not at the ground.

- **Remember you're not the center of (other people's) attention** – you may feel like everyone is watching you, but they have their own lives and worries and are probably not nearly as interested in you as you think.

- **Ignore the naysayers** – don't seek external approval, you know yourself better than anyone else. Confidence and bravery come from within.

'We delight in the beauty of the butterfly, but rarely admit the changes it has gone through to achieve that beauty.'

Maya Angelou

STAND UP STRAIGHT

Do you frequently find yourself hunched over? Do you tend to stare at your feet rather than making eye contact, or look at the ground when you walk rather than engaging with your surroundings? Do your shoulders have a tendency to knit together, as if trying to shield the rest of your body from some external threat?

Poor posture can indicate a lack of self-confidence, along with a desire to go unnoticed and avoid unwanted attention. On the other hand, people who walk with their head up and shoulders back tend to come across as more confident, approachable and relaxed. Addressing your posture is therefore an important step towards increasing your self-confidence. Not only will you feel better about yourself, it will encourage others to view you more positively too, further enhancing your self-esteem.

The Magic Thread

- Start by imagining there is an invisible thread which runs from the top of your head, down the back of your neck and vertically through your spine.

- Now imagine someone holding this thread above your head, gently pulling it tighter and tighter.

- As the thread tightens, notice your chin moving away from your chest and your vertebrae sliding into alignment. Feel your shoulders open and your chest expand as breath flows through you.

- The simple act of noticing the way you carry yourself and standing up straight, makes you feel stronger, taller, and more confident. And looking more confident is the first step to feeling more confident. Try to maintain this posture as you go about your daily activities.

Take off
THE MASK

In a sea full of sharks, it's hard to be a clownfish. In a world that extols conformity, it takes guts to be yourself.

Being authentic means having the confidence to be true to yourself; your own values, needs, feelings, beliefs and personality. What's more, authenticity is linked to personal happiness and healthy relationships. Authentic people don't change their behavior from one conversation to the next but remain genuine and grounded.

When we fail to be authentic, we hide what is most attractive about ourselves. So be honest, be humble, be unpretentious, and be yourself.

LITTLE ACTS OF
Authenticity

- **Develop your own passions** – explore your interests regardless of whether or not they're perceived to be 'cool.'

- **Be present** – give people your full attention without letting your mind wander. This shows sincerity.

- **Say what you really think** – rather than what you think others want to hear.

- **Listen to your inner voice** – trust your instinct rather than the voice of the crowd.

- **Don't be a chameleon** – resist the temptation to act or speak differently just to fit in with different groups of people, or situations.

Dress Bravely

The clothes we wear aren't simply a reflection of our personal tastes and fashion choices, they can also hold a mirror to our self-esteem. When we pay attention to our appearance, it helps us to feel good about ourselves and that confidence can translate into other areas of our lives, too. On the other hand, if we're feeling a bit low or insecure we may resort to baggy, dull clothes to avoid being noticed.

Try dressing with purpose, even if you don't feel like it, and see if you feel more confident. You don't need to be a fashionista or a model, just rock your style with pride and see where it takes you.

DRESS TO

Impress

- Wear something red – the color red is said to be energizing.

- Wear a t-shirt with a funny slogan, or a statement designed to get people's attention.

- Wear something smart even if you don't need to and see how it makes you feel.

- If you're a woman, liberate yourself for a day or more by going braless.

- Go commando – no one will ever know!

DRESSED FOR

Battle

In case you're still wondering whether clothes really can be an act of bravery, check out these courageous souls.

- In 2018, a group of Iranian women dressed as men using wigs and fake facial hair, so that they could enter a football stadium (under Iranian law women are banned from attending football matches.) A photo of the disguised women went viral after it appeared on social media, with many people praising their bravery.

- Schoolboys in Exeter, UK, made the headlines after bravely dressing in skirts in protest at their school's uniform policy which banned them from wearing shorts in hot weather. Some of the boys even shaved their legs!

- In the early 1950s Christine Jorgensen became famous in the United States for transitioning from male to female and having sex reassignment surgery. The former soldier became an advocate for transgender people at a time when society adhered to strict notions of masculinity and femininity.

'Dressing is
a way of life.'

Yves Saint Laurent

LITTLE ACTS OF BRAVERY TO IMPROVE YOUR CONFIDENCE

- Have some professional photographs taken of yourself – bonus points if you can strip off to your underwear for a tasteful shoot that celebrates your body.

- Write a poem and share it with friends or post it on Facebook.

- Go to a music concert that's totally out of your comfort zone – it could be opera, heavy metal, anything you like, just as long as you wouldn't normally listen to it.

- Be a freegan for a day, or a week, and try dumpster-diving for food.

- Turn off your phone and other devices for 24 hours – it's amazing how many people find this hard to do.

- Dine alone in a restaurant.

Speak Bravely

Many of us find it difficult to ask for what we want, or express personal opinions. We shy away from awkward conversations and keep our views to ourself. But unless you make your wishes known, other people may remain oblivious to them. As the saying goes: 'if you don't ask, you don't get.'

What's more, finding the courage to voice our concerns or stand up for what we believe in is a crucial part of living bravely and authentically. Even if you're worried about putting your foot in it, or causing controversy, people are more likely to admire you when you respectfully state your case, than when you say nothing at all.

'I wanted you to see what real courage is, instead of getting the idea that courage is a man with a gun in his hand. It's when you know you're licked before you begin, but you begin anyway and see it through no matter what.'

Harper Lee, To Kill A Mockingbird

Little Acts

OF VERBAL BRAVERY

- **Say 'no'** – no two letters are more important for setting boundaries and letting people know that you won't be taken for granted.

- **Stop saying 'just'** – every time you start a conversation or an email with 'just wondering...' or 'just following up...' it undermines your authority and softens what you want to say. Just leave it out!

- **Don't apologize when you've done nothing wrong** – in the same way as the word 'just' diminishes what you want to say, the word 'sorry' makes you sound submissive, as if you're seeking permission. So quit with 'sorry to bother you...' and 'sorry to ask...' and save your apologies for when you really need them.

BE BRAVE, BE

Vocal

- If you see someone dropping litter on the ground, politely ask them to pick it up.

- Haggle over an item you want to buy.

- Try on an item of clothing in a shop and ask a salesperson to give you their opinion.

- If you order a disappointing meal in a restaurant, politely let the waiter know.

- If you are struggling with a heavy item ask a stranger for help. Likewise, offer a hand to others when they are weighed down.

Turn up the Volume

MORE LITTLE ACTS OF BRAVERY TO MAKE A NOISE ABOUT

- Give a speech on a subject you're passionate about.

- Take part in a karaoke session.

- Phone someone who owes you an explanation or an apology. Resist the temptation to email.

- Make a complaint in person about something you're unhappy with.

- Ask someone who's borrowed an item to return it.

BE BRAVE, BE

Vulnerable

It takes great strength to show weakness. Often, we are reluctant to share too much of ourselves, for fear of being judged or criticised.

Yet opening our hearts can be both liberating and powerful. It releases us from the weight of feeling like we constantly need to put a brave face on things and demonstrates our humanity to others.

Surrendering your defenses also enables you to connect more deeply with others, and to receive support and encouragement.

LITTLE ACTS OF BRAVE VULNERABILITY

- Share a personal story about yourself with someone you trust.

- Ask for help – whether you are struggling with addiction, loneliness or stress, support is out there.

- Share a heartfelt post on social media – it could be about something that keeps you up at night, or a source of personal sadness.

- Be honest in admitting when you don't know the answer to something.

- Own up to mistakes.

'It takes courage to grow up and become who you really are.'

E.E. Cummings

MORE LITTLE ACTS OF BRAVERY JUST FOR FUN

You're getting braver every day, so try these little acts of bravery, just because...

- Try a new food even if it sounds gross – chicken sushi anyone?

- Wear something you've never had the courage to wear before – a bikini, a crazy shirt, a smart suit, or maybe you've always wanted to dress as the opposite sex.

- Put on a different face – if you're a make-up queen, leave it off for a day. Or if you usually go au naturel, try wearing some brightly colored lippy for a change.

- Go hairy (or hairless) – if you're a man, grow a beard, or shave it off if you already have one. If you're a woman, go without shaving your legs or even your armpits (gasp!) for a few weeks.

- Climb a tree – who said tree-climbing is just for kids?

48

IF YOU'RE READY FOR A CHALLENGE, TRY THESE:

- **Ask someone out on a date** – or join a dating agency. Braver still, go speed-dating! If you are already in a relationship, make an unexpected romantic gesture.

- **Try a new activity that scares you** – how about a trapeze class or surfing?

- **Conquer a small fear** – hold a (non-venomous) spider in your hand, visit a reptile house, or look down from a tall building, as long as it's safe to do so.

- **Draw attention to yourself in public** – sing in the checkout line, dance in the street.

- **Have your five minutes of fame** – apply to be on a TV gameshow, sign up to be a film extra, or phone into your local radio station.

AND IF YOU'RE FEELING REALLY BRAVE, TRY THESE:

- Take a bus, train, or even a plane to a place you've never visited before, without making any plans for when you get there.

- Be a life-drawing model for an art class.

- Ask a stranger for their phone number.

- Go salsa dancing (even if you've never done it before) and dance with someone you've never met before.

- Get in touch with someone who used to intimidate you or put you down, a former teacher or an ex, for example, and let them know how well you're doing now.

Brave New Life

Now that you have located your inner warrior,
it's time to step boldly forwards into action
and put that bravery into practice in the
world of work, life and relationships.

Courage is the basis of success; without it we
are left with a series of excuses for why we
can't or shouldn't change. So remember:
life is as big as your dreams.

'You must never be fearful about what you are doing when it is right.'

Rosa Parks

EXPAND YOUR
Horizons

People often appear sorted; perhaps they have a nice house, a decent car, a secure job, a long-term relationship. But while they may appear to have everything sewn-up on the outside, it might just be that their lives are devoid of challenge. And maybe they're fine with that. Or maybe they're not.

Real bravery involves pushing yourself beyond the picket fence and the 9-5 and striving for the things that set your heart and mind on fire.

Sometimes, bravery involves questioning whether you're in the right job or the right relationship, or if you're really living the life you dreamt of as a child, or even last year. This section will help you ask and answer those questions and inspire you to make changes.

Ask Yourself

Bravery often starts with asking yourself what it is you really want in life. This could mean veering off the safe and narrow onto the road less-travelled, or even forging your own path. So go on, ask yourself...

- Are you happy with your life?

- Is there anything you'd like to change?

- What is stopping you living the life you want?

- How can you achieve your goals?

COMMON

Obstacles

In order to move forward, you need to identify what's holding you back. Do you recognize any of these common roadblocks?

- Perfectionism – if you wait for the perfect moment it may never come.

- Over-planning – there's nothing wrong with being prepared, except when it becomes a substitute for actually doing the thing you're preparing for.

- Self-doubt – if you didn't feel worried, it wouldn't be an act of bravery. Dig deep and tell yourself you can do it.

Aim High

If you could do anything, what would it be? Dare to create a vision for your life that is bigger than the one you currently have. Because unless you dream big, you'll never reach the sky.

What's more, unfulfilled desires and unchartered risks are just a recipe for regret. So have the guts to step boldly from your comfort zone and make the leap into the unknown. The greatest risk of all is to play it safe.

Use visualizations to help you work towards your target.

HAVE A GAME PLAN

You're more likely to achieve your dreams if you have a plan of action.

- Have a definite goal – for example, don't just say you want a new job, have a specific job in mind.

- Turn negatives into positives – focus on how you'll feel when you achieve your goal, instead of dwelling on what could go wrong.

- Give yourself a deadline – having a schedule keeps you focussed and gives you a time frame in which to act.

- Write it down – start a journal in which to write down all your ambitions.

- Make yourself accountable – telling other people about a goal makes it more real and provides an added incentive to make it happen.

Acts of Bravery

THAT COULD CHANGE YOUR LIFE

How many of these would you love to do? Don't let fear hold you back.

- Move to a new area, or even another country.

- Get out of an unhappy relationship, or find love.

- Take a gap year and go travelling, or volunteer overseas.

- Train in your dream career.

- Give up the rat race to do something more meaningful, or to spend time with people you care about.

- Start a family, or expand the one you've got.

- Take part in a challenging event such as climbing a mountain or running a marathon.

It takes courage to question the life you are currently living, but it also opens your mind to new possibilities.

Ultimately, being willing to take risks unlocks the door to a more exciting and meaningful life. The life you've always wanted.

Keep practising visualizations to keep you motivated and help your dreams to materialise.

'And the day came when the risk to remain tight in a bud was more painful than the risk it took to blossom.'

Elizabeth Appell

'THE WORST CASE SCENARIO'

Game

This is a good technique to try whenever you face a tough decision. The idea is to think of something you really want to do – such as emigrating to a new country or leaving your job – but don't yet have the courage to pursue. Then ask yourself: what is the worst thing that could possibly happen? Don't hold back, let your imagination have a party.

Although it sounds counterintuitive, we usually realize that the worst-case scenario is unlikely to happen, or is not that bad after all, and that we will at least survive.

What's more, should the worst happen, you're more prepared to deal with it, because you've already thought about it.

HOW IT WORKS

- Think of something you really want to change, then write down all the possible outcomes, however awful or ridiculous.

- For example, if you leave your job you might never find another one, you'll have no money and will end up living in a cardboard box.

- Now ask yourself: what are the chances of that actually happening? What would you do if it did happen? Hopefully, you will realize that there are plenty of more positive scenarios.

- Facing the unknown helps make it less frightening. You realize things are never as bad as you imagine and that you could deal with it.

- On the other hand, when you avoid considering the worst-case scenario, you increase the horror factor by placing it outside of your ability to cope.

BRAVERY IN THE WORKPLACE

For many of us, work is where we spend the majority of our time, at least when we're awake. Sadly, workplace stress is a major factor in triggering depression and anxiety, and record numbers of people are now taking time off sick due to poor mental health. If you are in a job that is making you ill or miserable, or taking over your life, it can take enormous courage to change things, but it could be the best decision you ever make. Sometimes, the bravest thing you can do is quit.

'Don't confuse having a career with having a life.'

Hillary Clinton

'Above all, don't fear difficult moments. The best comes from them.'

Rita Levi-Montalcini

STAND UP FOR YOUR WORKING RIGHTS

- **Go home on time** – many offices have a 'must be seen to work late' culture. By opposing this and leaving on time you'll help set a precedent for others to do the same. Of course, there will be occasions when this isn't possible – when you have an urgent deadline for example, or someone who depends on you. But these should be the exceptions, rather than the rule.

- **Take regular breaks** – as an employee you have the right to time out. So resist the urge to inhale a sandwich at your desk, and get outside, even if only for a few minutes. It will make you more productive in the long run, too.

- **Take sick days** – if you are genuinely ill, stay at home. There's no point dragging yourself to work sniffling and sneezing and medicated up to the eyeballs. And it's wrong of companies to expect this.

MORE ACTS OF BRAVERY IN THE

- **Ask for a promotion** – don't wait for your next review, just ask.

- **Request a pay-rise** – because you're worth more.

- **Share your triumphs** – whether it's great results or positive feedback from clients, don't hold back in letting others know, especially your boss.

- **Learn from your mistakes** – we all mess up; don't beat yourself up, just reflect on what went wrong and move on.

- **Speak to your boss about something that's bothering you** – unless you are the boss!

- **Speak out against the gender pay gap** – women and men who do the same job deserve to be paid the same.

'Never be afraid to be a poppy in a field of daffodils.'

Michaela DePrince

BRAVERY IN
Relationships

We all need people in our lives. Our relationships with family, friends, children and romantic partners bring meaning, joy and purpose to our existence – as long as those relationships are positive, healthy and mutual. Of course, even the best relationships can be testing at times, but to fear love is to fear humanity, and ultimately to fear ourselves.

'Love is what we are born with. Fear is what we learn.'

Marianne Williamson

LITTLE ACTS OF BRAVERY IN RELATIONSHIPS

- Love – some people are easier to love than others; it can take bravery to love people who have hurt us.

- Saying sorry – it takes bravery and humility to admit when you're wrong and courage to make amends.

- Forgiveness – forgiving others doesn't mean you have to accept what they've done but it can help you to move on. Sometimes, it's necessary to forgive people and let them go.

- Commitment – deciding to spend the rest of your life with someone or to have a family with them can be exhilarating and terrifying in equal measure.

- Openness – it takes bravery to share your deepest thoughts and feelings and to place your trust in someone, especially if you've been let down before.

- Compromise – just make sure you're not the only one doing the compromising.

'It takes a great deal of bravery to stand up to our enemies, but just as much to stand up to our friends.'

J. K Rowling

FREEDOM FROM TOXIC RELATIONSHIPS

Unfortunately, sometimes we find ourselves in relationships which bring us down rather than build us up and it can require a huge amount of courage to free ourselves from these relationships.

All relationships have their highs and lows but healthy ones recover whereas toxic ones only destroy, gnawing away at your self-esteem, taking you further away from yourself and other people in your life.

A toxic relationship doesn't have to be with a romantic partner, it could also be with a friend, relative or colleague. The one thing all toxic people have in common is that they dominate and control, dragging you down while disregarding your feelings and needs.

It takes enormous courage to leave a toxic relationship. If you feel threatened, afraid or controlled in any way, don't hesitate in seeking help.

BREAKING UP IS HARD TO DO

There is no denying that ending a serious relationship is one of life's most heartbreaking events. You may share a home, children, bank accounts, pets, friends and so much more. Breaking up with someone can literally turn your life upside down, and it's for this reason that many couples stay together even when they're unhappy.

However, while breaking up is always painful, the alternative of remaining in a destructive relationship is usually far worse.

'If you're brave enough to say goodbye, life will reward you with a new hello.'

Paulo Coelho

THE COURAGE TO SAY

Goodbye

Even when you're certain that a relationship is broken beyond repair, it takes great strength to walk away. You will need courage to:

- accept that it's over.

- face things head on.

- be prepared for things to get worse before they get better.

- understand that you may lose more than just your partner.

- have faith that you will move on.

- know beyond doubt that it's better to break up than to spend your life with the wrong person.

Brave New World

The great thing about bravery is that it doesn't stop with ourselves. Once you've discovered the power of bravery for yourself, you can start using it to help others, too. From sticking up for the underdog to saving someone's life, this section will help you channel your courage as a force for good in the world.

'If you are neutral in situations of injustice, you have chosen the side of the oppressor. If an elephant has its foot on the tail of a mouse, and you say that you are neutral, the mouse will not appreciate your neutrality.'

Desmond Tutu

BRAVERY VERSUS

Bullying

Sadly, in today's world, bullying is all too common in schools, workplaces and homes. Ideally, we would be able to combat bullying through kindness. By showing the bullies a better way we would soften their hearts and change their actions forever. Yet, unfortunately, love doesn't always win and sometimes bravery is the only option. By standing up to the haters and speaking out on behalf of those who suffer, we can create a climate of zero-tolerance.

LITTLE ACTS OF ANTI-BULLYING

- **Don't be a bystander** – in the past a bit of conflict was seen as 'character building', but gone are the days of turning a blind eye. It's now recognized that bullying can have a devastating effect on the social, emotional and even physical wellbeing of victims.

- **Intervene** – taking a stand against bullies, or stepping in on someone's behalf may not be easy, but it's becoming increasingly important in today's society and could even save a life.

- **Support the victim** – this could be as simple as encouraging them to report the bullying, or accompanying them as they do so.

- **Be sympathetic** – let the victim know how sorry you are that they are being bullied.

- **Make kindness the norm** – if everyone did this, bullying wouldn't exist. Bravely model kind behavior, always.

'When you hear people making hateful comments, stand up to them. Point out what a waste it is to hate, and you could open their eyes.'

Taylor Swift

STAND UP TO

Cyberbullying

The internet provides unprecedented opportunities for bullying and teenagers are especially vulnerable. Cyberbullying is considered abusive behavior by almost every website's terms of service.

It's just as important not to be a bystander online, as it is in any other situation.

'The world is a dangerous place, not because of those who do evil, but because of those who look on and do nothing.'

Albert Einstein

Little Acts

OF BRAVERY ONLINE

- If you come across people talking badly about someone online, or sending abusive messages, report their account. There is an option for this on most social media websites.

- Remind people to think before they post. If someone you know wants to call someone out on social media, ask them to consider the consequences.

- Remind people that once something is on the internet it's there forever.

- If you see others making unkind comments about someone online, respond with something positive about that person.

BE AN ENCOURAGER

In a world full of critics, stand out from the crowd by building up the people around you. If you hear people gossiping, don't be drawn in; instead challenge them by interjecting with something nice.

'Strong people don't put others down. They lift them up.'

Michael P. Watson

It takes bravery to speak out, but the words we use can have the power to make or break someone's self-esteem, so choose wisely and be an orator of positivity and encouragement.

What's more, showing someone that you believe in them can give them the confidence to believe in themselves, too.

CONGRATULATE THE WINNER (EVEN WHEN IT HURTS)

It's one thing to say 'well done' when our own pride isn't at stake, but it takes strength to applaud the success of our competitors: the colleague who got the promotion, the classmate who got top marks, the person who ran faster, scored more goals or earned more money, the parent whose child won the trophy.

Genuinely applauding the success of our rivals not only helps override hard feelings, but demonstrates personal bravery. Anyone can be successful, but not everyone has the courage to lose.

'Courage is the discovery that you may not win and trying when you know you can lose.'

Tom Krause

BLOW YOUR OWN
Trumpet

Everyone is good at something, so own your talents! Acknowledging your skills or gifts isn't about bragging, it's about having the self-confidence to recognize your strengths.

Many of us cringe at the idea of self-promotion, but the fact is if you don't do it yourself no-one else is going to do it for you. And as long as you don't trample over others in the process, flying your own kite is often the only way to get where you want to be in life.

'You are braver than you believe, stronger than you seem, and smarter than you think.'

AA Milne

PUT YOURSELF

Out There

You've owned your talents, (softly) blown your own trumpet, now it's time to demonstrate your capabilities to the outside world. What's more, everyone wins – other people will enjoy the fruits of your talents and you'll become even more confident through their approval.

Here are some things you could try:

- Musically gifted – put on a recital for the residents of a nursing home, or go busking. Bonus points if you apply to go on a talent show!

- Baking fingers – start selling your creations as a side-hustle. Who knows, it could even lead to a new career.

- Good with words or pictures – start a blog or instagram account.

- Successful career – offer to give a talk at a local school to inspire students. Even if it sounds daunting, you never know who might be grateful in the future.

- Great at making people laugh – have a go at being a stand-up comedian. Start with local gigs and see where it takes you.

GIANT ACTS OF BRAVERY TOWARDS OTHERS

Give a Kidney

Some acts of bravery are so huge, they can only be described as heroic – and this is one of them! If you have two healthy kidneys, you may be able to donate one of them to save someone else's life. The number of people waiting for kidneys is far greater than the number of kidneys that become available each year, so by deciding to become a living donor you could completely transform someone's life.

You don't even need to know anyone waiting for a transplant as you can sign up to donate a kidney to a stranger, also known as non-directed donation.

HOW IT WORKS

Before donating, you'll be asked to undergo lots of tests to make sure you are healthy enough and are sure that you want to go ahead. If you do decide to donate, you'll be able to lead a perfectly healthy life with just one kidney – and the knowledge that you really have saved a life. Contact your nearest transplant centre if you'd like to know more.

'When beauty shines from within there can be no denying it.'

Alek Wek

Sometimes miracles are just people with kind hearts.

ACTS OF BRAVERY FOR

Women Only

It's almost impossible to understand the agony of longing for a child but being unable to have one, unless you have been in that position. Yet thanks to the incredible bravery and compassion that exists in the world, there is hope for parents-in-waiting who have been dealt an unkind hand of fate.

LEND YOUR WOMB

If you are a healthy woman who is able to carry a baby to full term, you may be able to act as a surrogate for another woman who is desperate for a child but unable to carry one herself. It could be someone close to you, or someone you haven't yet met. Either way, this is another undeniably courageous act, with huge implications. Get in touch with an established surrogacy organization to discuss your options if you're interested.

DONATE YOUR EGGS

Egg donation involves going through part of the IVF process so that doctors can collect some of your eggs to help a woman who doesn't have viable eggs of her own, or couples who carry a genetic condition.

Often, women donate eggs to someone they know. But you can also donate anonymously, to help an infertile couple achieve their longed-for family.

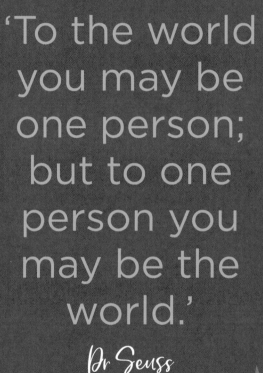

'To the world you may be one person; but to one person you may be the world.'

Dr Seuss

Face Your Own Mortality

DONATE YOUR BODY

Most of us don't like to dwell on our own mortality. Yet the fact is we are all going to die. Facing this certainty with bravery can help reduce the fear of dying and help others in the future.

Signing up to the organ donation register costs nothing and could save a life. Or you could consider leaving your body as a gift for a medical school. Such donations are a valuable resource for training and research. Most donated bodies are used for the teaching and perfecting of medical knowledge and techniques, helping to improve the care and treatment of future patients.

Donors are usually older people, as younger people are more likely to be eligible for the transplant scheme, but the decision takes bravery and kindness. Contact a medical school if you would like further information.

'Nothing in life is to be feared. It is only to be understood.'

Marie Curie

FINAL ACTS OF BRAVERY FOR A

Bold New Life

Your inner warrior is ready to burst forth. It's time to dig deep, throw on your armour and gallop towards your dreams. And when fear bites, remember the following:

- Stand firm and speak your truth – don't back down when others contradict your true values and beliefs.

- Accept responsibility – you have the power to decide whether to let the world affect you, or whether to have an effect on your world.

- Lean on others – courage is shared; draw strength from others and let them take strength from you.

- When in doubt, fake it – pretend to be braver than you feel and in doing so you will become braver than you were before.

- Persevere – being brave doesn't mean there won't be setbacks. Real bravery involves overcoming failures, picking yourself up and trying again. Remember, it's not just about reaching your goals, but having the courage to try. So don't give up!

'The only thing we have to fear is fear itself.'

Franklin D. Roosevelt